W9-BVP-254

Good Cooking for the Kidney Disease Diet

50 Recipes for the Renal Diet Cookbook

BY

Gordon Rock

Copyright 2015 Gordon Rock

License Notes

No part of this Book can be reproduced in any form or by any means including print, electronic, scanning or photocopying unless prior permission is granted by the author.

All ideas, suggestions and guidelines mentioned here are written for informative purposes. While the author has taken every possible step to ensure accuracy, all readers are advised to follow information at their own risk. The author cannot be held responsible for personal and/or commercial damages in case of misinterpreting and misunderstanding any part of this Book

About the author

Gordon Rock is the author for hundreds of cookbooks on delicious meals that the 'average Joe' can attempt at home. Including, but definitely not limited to, the Amazon Prime bestseller "Smoking Meat: The Essential Guide to Real Barbecue".

Rock is also known for other well-known titles such as "Making Fresh Pasta", "Hot Sauce", "The Paleo Chocolate Lovers" and "Vegan Tacos", just to name a few.

Rock has been nominated for various awards and has recently been offered a 'Question & Answers' column in Food and Wine Magazine that will give him a greater medium to respond to all the queries readers may have after attempting his recipes. He has also been honored by the

Institution of Culinary Excellence for his outstanding recipes.

Gordon Rock grew up in the outskirts of Los Angeles in California, where he graduated from the Culinary Institute of America with honors. He still resides there along with his wife and three kids. He operates a non - profit organization for aspiring cooks who are unable to finance their culinary education and spends practically all his spare time either in the kitchen or around his desk writing.

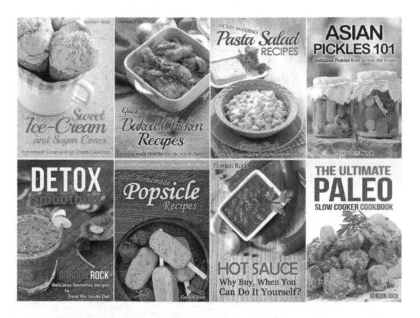

For a complete list of my published books, please, visit my Author's Page...

http://amazon.com/author/gordonrock

You can also check out my blog at: http://grodon-rock.blogspot.com

Or my Facebook Page at: https://www.facebook.com/ChefGordonRock

Table of Contents

Introduction

Believe it or not, being told that you must go on the renal diet is not a culinary death sentence. I have been on it for almost ten years now and have come to understand a few things. While it does bring forth some dietary changes and giving up somethings it is not, by any means, the end of flavor. Balance is the key to enjoying meals and the best way to achieve that is through the foods natural flavors.

That's what Good Cooking for the Kidney Disease Diet: 50 Recipes for the Renal Diet Cookbook is all about! Its goal is to widen your culinary horizons and have you creating tasty meals that make you want to eat!

So grab your copy of Good Cooking for the Kidney Disease Diet: 50 Recipes for the Renal Diet Cookbook today and start cooking, and enjoying, meals throughout the day!

Breakfast

Eating a well-rounded, protein laden breakfast plays an important part in determining the quality of your day. In this chapter there are recipes to fit into and help shape the day's intake and parameters. As each day presents its own unique challenges and needs you will find here ten recipes that can easily be modified or enjoyed as is and paired with the other recipes within this book!

Steak and Eggs on a Bed of Spinach

A great dish to start the day! 1 serving

Ingredients:

- 1 breakfast, sandwich, or thin steak, 4 oz. 2 tablespoon olive oil
- 1 cup spinach
- 1 cup diced tomatoes
- 1/2 teaspoon lemon juice
- 1 dash red pepper flakes
- 2 eggs or egg substitute

Directions:

Marinade the steak in 1 tablespoon of olive oil and red pepper flakes overnight to tenderize. Dice steak or cut into strips and cook in a skillet 30-40 seconds to avoid toughness.

In separate pot with 1 tablespoon of olive oil and over medium high heat cook spinach, tomatoes, and lemon juice; last, add steak pieces to spinach mixture and stir together.

Cook eggs sunny side up and ladle spinach mixture over it.

Nutritional Information:

- Sodium: 95 mg
- Potassium: 560.6
- Calcium: 49.6
- Protein: 37.3

Microwave French Toast Casserole

A quick way to get a protein boost! Great for brunch or a snack! To better control the ingredients in your bread, especially the sodium, consider making your bread.

Makes 1 cup

Ingredients:

- 2 cups cubed white bread
- 3 oz. turkey breakfast sausage
- 1 egg or egg substitute equivalent to 1 egg
- 2 cups coconut milk
- 2 teaspoon cinnamon

Directions:

In small bowl mix together egg, half and half, cinnamon, and nutmeg. Place bread cubes into casserole dish and coat with egg mixture; cook 1 minute then if needed cook in 10 second increments. Meanwhile, in a skillet or small pot cook turkey sausage according to directions on the package; if necessary, place cooked sausage on paper towel covered plate, let drain and when ready pour on top of French toast.

 The sausage can be cooked in the microwave on top of the French toast; it is a matter of personal taste.

Nutritional Information:

- Sodium: 743.6 mg
- Potassium: 354.8 mg
- Calcium: 105.3 mg
- Protein: 20.5 g

Zesty Pancakes

Throw in your favorite veggies and make it a brunch!

Makes 4 small-medium sized pancakes

Ingredients:

- 3/4 cup all-purpose flour
- 1 egg
- 1/2 cup milk or non-dairy creamer
- 1 tablespoon hot water
- 1 teaspoon orange peel

Directions:

In mixing bowl stir together all ingredients, if mixture is to thick add more water 1 tsp at a time. Heat burner to medium-high heat and pour mixture onto hot griddle and let cook 3-5 minutes on each side.

Nutritional Information:

- Figured using ½ cup 2% milk
- Sodium: 57 mg
- Potassium: 321.2 mg
- Calcium: 184.8 mg
- Protein: 21.7 g

Egg Casserole

Makes for a quick and easy but filling breakfast!

Makes 6 - 1 cup servings

Ingredients:

- 1/2 cup English muffin cubes
- 2 egg or egg substitute
- 1 teaspoon thyme leaves
- 1 teaspoon pepper
- 1/2 spinach or broccoli
- 1/3 cup diced bell pepper or red pepper flakes
- 3 oz. turkey sausage, pork sausage or 3 oz. low sodium diced ham
- 1/4 cup cheddar cheese

Directions:

Prepare 9x9 casserole dishes and preheat oven to 350. On the bottom of the casserole dish place a layer of English muffin cubes and in a separate bowl mix together eggs, thyme, and pepper and pour on top of muffin pieces. Top with sausage and cheese; cook 18-22 minutes.

Nutritional Information:

- Figured with turkey sausage
- Sodium: 296 mg
- Potassium: 248.7 mg
- Calcium: 122.6 mg
- Protein: 14.4 g

Egg Muffins

Great for on-the-go breakfast or an impromptu brunch! The bigger size allows you to pack them with more nutrients!

Makes 6

Ingredients:

- 3 eggs or egg substitute
- 1/4 cup milk or non-dairy creamer
- 3 oz. turkey breakfast sausage
- 1 teaspoon parsley (optional)
- 1 teaspoon turmeric (optional)

Directions:

Preheat oven to 350 and prepare muffin pan. Beat eggs and add to mix other ingredients and additions, fill ½ to 2/3 full and bake for 10-12 minutes.

Nutritional Information:

- Sodium: 245 mg
- Potassium: 255 mg
- Calcium: 143.4 mg
- Protein: 18.6 g

10 minute Protein Bites

These are excellent for a quick way to get your morning dose of protein that can easily be fixed to your liking. Stack these bites full of your favorite veggies and spices or use them as a quick way to appease your guest dietary needs without spending hours in the kitchen! Also a great way to incorporate small doses of meats while measurements; foods such as certain hams and bacon. Let your imagination run wild with these bites and use them for various meals!

The nutritional information below is based up the use of a 12 mold pan each filled 1/2 - 2/3 full. Remember to fill all unused molds with water to promote even cooking. Makes 9-12

- 10-12 eggs scrambled

Preheat oven to 325 and prepare pan. Best if eggs are mixed in a measuring cup or bowl with a lip for ease of pouring; add any spices and pour into molds, fill with any veggies, cheeses, or meats. Bake 8 - 10 minutes.

Nutritional Information:

For 12 eggs:

- Sodium: 648 mg
- Potassium: 628.8 mg
- Calcium: 766.8 mg
- Protein: 57.6 g

Tex-Mex Breakfast Burrito

Great way to get creative with the leftovers and spices!

Makes 1

Ingredients:

- 1 10 inch burrito wrap
- 2 scrambled eggs or liquid egg substitute
- 1 tablespoon button mushroom pieces, diced
- 1 teaspoon salsa

Directions:

With sauce brush lightly coat both sides of tortilla and warm over medium high heat (Warming helps to keep it from breaking, the duration of cooking it is a matter of personal taste, for extra flavor sprinkle you fav. No-salt seasonings in the oil then coat the tortillas. (Turmeric is a great compliment to salsa).

In skillet over medium high heat scramble two eggs, let cook thirty seconds and add the turmeric, salsa, and mushrooms. Mix together well, spoon into the middle of tortilla, wrap and serve.

Nutritional Information:

- Sodium: 402 mg
- Potassium: 122.2 mg
- Calcium: 120.8 mg
- Protein: 12.7 g

Steak and Eggs To Go

Great for busy mornings or anytime snacks!

Makes 6

Ingredients:

- 2 pieces breakfast steak (not to exceed 3 oz.), diced
- 3 scrambled eggs
- 1 dash black pepper or red pepper flakes
- 1 teaspoon chopped basil

Directions:

Prepare square brownie molds or 9x9 dish and preheat oven to 350. In a bowl mix together diced steak, scrambled eggs, pepper, and basil. Pour into squares, filling the empties with water, and bake 10-12 minutes.

Nutritional Information:

- Sodium: 237 mg
- Potassium: 156.8 mg
- Calcium: 67 mg
- Protein: 28 g

Spicy Egg Bowl

Add spinach or your fav meats and load up on protein!

Makes 12 bowls

Ingredients:

- 6 corn tortillas
- 5-6 eggs or egg substitute scrambled
- 1 tablespoon chopped parsley
- 1 tablespoon finely diced onion

Directions:

Fix bowls and preheat oven to 350. In a bowl scramble eggs along with parsley and onion; fill bowls 1/2 - 2/3 full and bake 10-13 minutes.

Nutritional Information:

Based on 6 corn tortillas and 5 eggs

- Sodium: 301 mg
- Potassium: 267 mg
- Calcium: 73 mg
- Protein: 30.4 g

Breakfast Salad

Kale is high in iron so this breakfast is a great way to get extra iron!

Makes 1 salad

Ingredients:

- 1 cup kale
- 4-6 grape tomatoes
- 1 tablespoon olive oil or lemon juice.

Directions:

Mix kale and tomatoes together, cover with olive oil or lemon juice.

Nutritional Information:

- Sodium: 31 mg
- Potassium: 342 mg
- Calcium: 94 mg
- Protein: 4 g

Lunch

Lunch can be a tricky meal. You want to keep up the dietary needs to power through the remaining day, but you don't want to use up your allowance before dinners or snacks. Within these chapters are ten recipes of various numerical parameters to try to fit in with your needs. Otherwise, they serve as great templates to help you get where you need to be!

Teriyaki-Honey Ginger Salmon and Bean Casserole

Turmeric can get hot when used in large doses, so either beware or pile it on depending on you heat tolerance! Turmeric is the main spice in curries to give you an idea of the heat levels of this fine spice. It is a root spice, like ginger, so is all natural and excellent to add a strong flavor to your foods. However, if you are purchasing it from a supermarket make sure to check the ingredients; this might require some internet searching. The goal is to get it, or any spice, in it's most natural and pure form. Also, turmeric can stain unless wiped up or washed away in a timely fashion!

Makes 4-6 servings

Ingredients:

- 1 fillet of wild caught salmon (shrimp is a viable substitute just be sure to clean it!)
- 1 tablespoon Honey
- 1 tablespoon Worcester sauce
- 2 tablespoon dry white wine or white cooking wine
- 4 tablespoon olive oil, divided
- 1 teaspoon turmeric (for more, add one teaspoon at a time)
- 1/2 teaspoon fresh grated ginger or 1 teaspoon powder ginger
- 1 teaspoon onion powder
- 114.5 oz. can of no salt green beans, drained
- 1 14.5 oz. can of no or low salt can of sliced potatoes, drained

- 1/2 cup strips of bell pepper (red is best but use whatever you have on hand)

TIP: If you cannot find no or low salt foods you can always toss them under cold water for 2-3 minutes to remove the seasonings. For low or no salt foods we suggest toss them in a colander under cold water 45 seconds - 1 minute to ensure the lowest possible salt content.

Directions:

Marinate the fish in honey, Worcester sauce, wine, and 2 tablespoons olive oil 8 hours - overnight. Empty contents of fish marinade into Dutch oven or large pot and cook until flakey but not thoroughly done, approximately 30 -45 seconds and shred.

In Dutch oven mix together 2 tablespoon olive oil, turmeric, ginger, and onion powder; then, pour in dried green beans, peppers, and potatoes. Stir well, some of the potatoes may turn a yellow-red-orange color this is fine.

Let simmer on medium-low a few more minutes and pour into large serving dish.

Nutritional Information:

- Sodium: 302 mg
- Potassium: 659.8 mg
- Calcium: 28 mg
- Protein: 50 g

Ham Sandwich Wraps

Good source of protein to carry you through to dinner!
When shopping for lunch meats always check labels, even
for the packages that say low sodium. What's low for some
might not be low enough for you. Ham can be especially
high in sodium so enquire about various brands at the deli.

Makes: 1 serving

Ingredients:

- 1 6.5 inch low salt pita round
- 1 slice low sodium ham
- 1/2 cup bok choy, diced
- 1 carrot diced or cut into matchsticks
- 1/2 cup Home-made Vinaigrette dressing (see below for recipe)

Home-Made Vinaigrette: *Approx. 1 cup*

- 1/2 cup olive oil
- 1/3 cup red wine vinegar
- 1 teaspoon rosemary, finely chopped
- 1 teaspoon thyme, finely chopped
- 1 teaspoon oregano, finely chopped
- 1 teaspoon basil, finely chopped
- 1/2 teaspoon minced garlic
- 1/2 teaspoon red pepper flakes

Directions:

In large mixing bowl stir together bok choy, carrots, and 1/2 cup of home-made dressing, if not using the other half it will keep for 3-5 days in an airtight container in the refrigerator. Shake before serving. On a flat surface lay out on pita round and fill with 1 slice of ham and bok choy mixture.

Nutritional Information:

- Sodium: 559 mg
- Potassium: 201 mg
- Calcium: 63.3
- Protein: 26 g

Turkey Burger on Ciabatta with Sweet Potato Wedges

Turkey is higher in protein and lower in fat then most hamburgers. Lean meats, such as poultry and fish, are always the better choice for CKD and ESRD patients.

Makes 1 serving

Ingredients:

- 1 ciabatta roll
- 1 turkey burger (4 oz.)
- 1 teaspoon brown sugar
- 1 teaspoon thyme leaves
- 1 onion 1/4 of it cut into rounds and 1/4 diced
- 1 large sweet potato cut into wedges (4 oz.)
- 2 tablespoon of garlic and parsley

Directions:

Wash thoroughly sweet potato even if labeled organic. Cut into wedges and steam along with 1/4 diced onions next lay them out on a flat surface and sprinkle with seasoning.

While the potato wedges are cooling mix together in a small bowl brown sugar and thyme and smear unto uncooked turkey burger.

Cook burger according to directions seasoning should not affect cooking time.

If desired toast bun but this is not necessary and place turkey burger along with a few onions rounds on it.

Nutritional Information:

- Sodium: 814 mg
- Potassium: 446 mg
- Calcium: 53 mg
- Protein: 31 g

Chicken Pot Pie Muffins

A creative way to use up leftovers!

Makes 4-6

Ingredients:

- 1 package phylo dough
- 4 oz. boneless skinless chicken breast, cooked and shredded
- 1 cup cooked white rice
- 1/3 cup drained and washed low or no sodium garbanzo beans
- 1 tablespoon
- 1 teaspoon garlic and parsley seasoning
- 1 finely chopped basil leaf

Directions:

Prepare muffin molds and preheat oven to 375; in a bowl mix together chicken, rice, beans, and seasonings. Lay dough on floured flat surface and cut dough into to circles to fit inside muffin holes.

Fill each muffin with a large spoonful of mixture and cover with dough circle. Piece top with fork a few times or create 2 1-2 inch slits to allow steam to escape. Cook 18-22 minutes.

Nutritional Information:

- Sodium: 371 mg
- Potassium: 414.7 mg
- Calcium: 57.6 mg
- Protein: 43.6 g

Fillet of Cod Pita

Works with all types of fish, makes 1 serving

Ingredients:

- 3 oz. cod fillet (*will shrink when cooked)
- 1 small pita pocket halved
- Olive oil
- 1 teaspoon smoky paprika
- 1/4 teaspoon black pepper
- 1 tablespoon Worcester sauce
- 2 basil leaves

Directions:

Thaw, drain, dry, and otherwise prepare cod. Sprinkle with paprika and pepper and in skillet over medium high heat with 1 teaspoon olive oil cook cod until flaky.

Drizzle inside of both pita half with olive oil, remove fish and place in between pita halves and stick basil on top of fish. Stick sandwich back into skillet; cook 1-2 minutes on each side.

Nutritional Information:

- Sodium: 288 mg
- Potassium: 386 mg
- Calcium: 71 mg
- Protein: 26.2

Baked Chicken Nuggets in a Veggie Salad

Great snacks for all to enjoy!

Makes 10-12 nuggets

Ingredients:

- 3 oz. boneless skinless chicken breast or thighs, cubed 2x2
- 3 eggs
- Salt free breadcrumbs
- No-salt herb seasoning
- 3 oz. bell pepper strips
- 1/4 cup diced water chestnuts
- 1 stalk chopped bok choy
- 1 can 3-4 oz. beansprouts

Directions:

Prepare baking tray with parchment paper or aluminum foil and preheat oven to 375. In one bowl scramble egg mixture, in second mix together breadcrumbs and seasoning; dredge chicken through egg coating both sides and then through the breadcrumbs thoroughly coating both sides. Lay 2 inches apart on tray and cook 22-27 minutes.

* Under cooked chicken can be hazardous to your health so be sure to cut into a piece checking for any running juices or pink meat before consuming. A longer cooking time or higher oven temp might be needed. In a bowl toss together peppers, water chestnuts, bok choy, and beansprouts. Drizzle with a low sodium Asian dressing.

Nutritional Information:

- Sodium: 72 mg
- Potassium: 248 mg
- Calcium: 24 mg
- Protein: 28 g

Shrimp Pizza

Works with chicken too!

Makes 1 pizza, serves 4

Ingredients:

- 1 cup salad shrimp
- 1/3 cup cherry tomatoes, halved
- 1 stalk bok choy, diced
- 1 cup spinach leaves
- 1/3 cup matchstick carrots
- 1/3 cup mozzarella or parmesan cheese
- 1 teaspoon red pepper flakes
- 1 tablespoon coarsely chopped basil leaves
- 1 1/2 teaspoon thyme leaves
- 1 low sodium or no sodium small pizza shell, pizza dough, or flatbread

Directions:

As when constructing any pizza, let each ingredient be a layer on which you build your pizza. Bake according to package directions.

Nutritional Information:

- Sodium: 162 mg
- Potassium: 300.3 mg
- Calcium: 165 mg
- Protein: 23 g

Irish Pub Burger's

To cut better nutritional numbers cut out the molasses and celery salt!

Makes 1 burger with sauce

Ingredients:

- 3 oz. lean hamburger
- 1 tablespoon chopped onion

Sauce:

- 1/2 cup molasses
- 1/3 cup ketchup
- 1/3 cup mustard
- 1 dash celery salt or celery flakes
- 2 chopped basil leaves (fresh or dried)

Directions:

In sauce pan over med.-low heat add all of the sauce ingredients together, stir well and let simmer for 30 minutes. Remove from heat and let sit in refrigerator until ready to use. Stir before putting on anything or using as a dip, it will keep 3-5 days in refrigerator if kept in an air tight container.

In a large bowl and using your hands mix together burger and onion and form into a patty or patties. Cook on stovetop grill or outdoor grill.

Nutritional Information:

- Sodium: 875 mg
- Potassium: 371.3 mg
- Calcium: 56 mg
- Protein: 21 g

Turkey Burger Quesadilla

Flour tortillas can be high in sodium and phosphorous, so be sure to read nutritional labels? Generic brands are often lower in salt and additives or consider making your own!

Makes 1 burger

Ingredients:

- 2 10 inch burrito tortilla
- 3 oz. turkey burger
- 1/4 cup cheddar cheese or Mexican blend
- 1/2 -3 /4 cup scallions
- 2 teaspoons chili powder
- 1/2 teaspoon cumin Or 1 tablespoon Mrs. Dash Mexican seasoning in lieu of chili powder and cumin

Directions:

Layer ingredients around 1 tortilla shell and lay the other on top when done. Make sure the cheese can easily reach both shells as it will act like glue when melted and keep the entire thing together. Cut in half or into 4th's before serving.

Nutritional Information:

- Sodium: 341 mg
- Potassium: 181 mg
- Calcium: 163 mg
- Protein: 23 g

Turkey Wraps

These can be made in advance, just wrap in plastic wrap or put in a baggie and you'll have protein packed lunch treats or mid-afternoon snacks ready to grab and go!

Makes 1 wrap

Ingredients:

- 1 sandwich wrap
- 3 oz. leftover turkey pieces or sliced turkey
- 1 tablespoon lite onion dip
- 1/3 cup diced bok choy or cucumber
- 1 teaspoon no salt seasoning
- 1 dash pepper or red pepper flakes

Directions:

Layout wrap and spread onion dip evenly on it. Layer remaining ingredients, roll together, refrigerate until ready to serve.

Nutritional Information:

- Sodium: 366 mg
- Potassium: 85.3
- Calcium: 80 mg
- Protein: 12 g

Dinner

Hopefully, by the time you reach dinner the bulk of the day's activities are done and you can start to wind down. Unfortunately, in today's world this is not always the case and dinner is just another stop for protein. This chapter brings you ten recipes that help you to rekindle your love for tasty eats while staying with your intake allowances!

London Broil with Spiced Rice

London broil's are low in vitamins but offer a decent dose of vitamin c so you don't have to worry about hidden additions unless clearly stated on the packing or found during your research. Paired with ginger, cauliflower, or other fruits and vegetables that are high in iron this would be a great meal when trying to overcome a cold or attempting to boost your immune system. 1 serving

Ingredients:

- 3 oz. London broil
- 3 oz. cauliflower rice
- 1 basil leaf chopped
- 2 tablespoon olive oil (coconut oil if watching your fat intake)
- 1 teaspoon fresh ginger root grated or minced
- 1 cup spinach

Directions:

Marinate London broil overnight in olive oil, ginger, and basil. Using a grater or a food processor pulse in short rapid burst until cauliflower is in rice six pieces cauliflower into rice size pieces.

In Dutch oven empty contents of marinade including London broil, and cook for thirty minutes then shred. Let cook 15 more minutes and add into pot cauliflower rice and spinach; mix together and let cook another 15 minutes. Serve.

Nutritional Information:

- Sodium: 129 mg
- Potassium: 430 mg
- Calcium: 56 mg
- Protein: 25 g

Beef and Broccoli Burritos

Easily converts into a casserole or crockpot meal!

Makes 2

Ingredients:

- 1 cup cooked rice
- 1 teaspoon olive oil
- 3 oz. shredded or beef strips
- 1/2 cup broccoli trees
- 1/3 cup sliced carrots
- Olive oil
- 1 teaspoon chili powder with extra
- 1 dash cumin
- 1/2 cup water
- 2 burrito tortillas

Directions:

In a Dutch oven over medium heat and 1 /2 teaspoon olive oil, chili powder, and cumin cook steak to desired doneness; add in cooked rice, broccoli, and carrots. Pour in 1/2 cup water, stir well, and reduce heat to low.

Warm skillet and layout one or two burritos, using a sauce brush paint coat one side of tortilla with olive oil and sprinkle a tiny bit of chili pepper into it; let cook 1-2 minutes per side. Remove to plate and fill with beef and broccoli mix.

Nutritional Information:

- Sodium: 423 mg
- Potassium: 315 mg
- Calcium: 149 mg
- Protein: 27 g

Seafood Stuffed Peppers

A great dish for special occasions!

Makes 4

Ingredients:

- 3 oz. shrimp, cleaned and de-tailed
- 2 cups cooked rice
- 4 bell peppers, washed with seeds removed
- 1 tablespoon shallot
- 1/2 cup bok choy
- 1 teaspoon turmeric

Directions:

Prepare 9x9 casserole dish for baking and preheat oven to 350.

In a food processor mix together shrimp and rice with a few quick pulses and empty into bowl, stir in bok choy and turmeric.

Spoon mixture in peppers and place into oven-ready casserole dish. Bake 25-30 minutes.

Nutritional Information:

- Sodium: 115 mg
- Potassium: 202.7
- Calcium: 106 mg
- Protein: 28 g

Chicken Ranch Casserole

Great for those hectic nights when there never seems to be enough time!

Makes 6 serving in 5 quart crockpot

Ingredients:

- 1 boneless, skinless chicken breast or thigh
- 1/2 tablespoon olive oil
- 1/2 cup water
- 1/3 cup dry white wine or cooking white wine
- 1/2 tablespoon finely diced mint leaves
- 2 teaspoon chili powder
- 1 teaspoon red pepper flakes
- 1 teaspoon thyme
- 2 cup uncooked rice

Directions:

Except for the uncooked rice cook chicken and all ingredients in crockpot on high for 30 minutes. Take chicken out, shred, and return, Add uncooked rice to chicken in crockpot and cook together on high 1-2.5 hours.

Nutritional Information:

- Sodium: 70 mg
- Potassium: 340 mg
- Calcium: 48mg
- Protein: 37 g

Chicken Teriyaki Stir-fry

Substitute snow peas for the green beans for a change!

Makes 1 serving

Ingredients:

- 3 oz. chicken cubes
- 2 teaspoon brown sugar
- 1/3 cup low sodium soy sauce
- 2 tablespoons raw organic honey
- 1 teaspoon low sodium sesame oil (optional)
- 1 cup cooked jasmine rice
- 1/2 cup no salt added green beans
- 1/3 cup baby corn

Directions:

In plastic bag marinate chicken cubes overnight in the refrigerator in brown sugar, soy sauce, honey, and sesame oil. Place into wok and cook until done; add rice, beans, and corn and warm through. Serve.

Nutritional Information:

- Sodium: 140 mg
- Potassium: 319 mg
- Calcium: 75.3 mg
- Protein: 37 g

Mini Taco Bowls

Check generic brands as they are usually lower in sodium. Also, the ethnic and Mexican/Latino sections of your store are usually full of items, spices, and seasonings that are lower in sodium. But for this recipes it will most likely be best to make your own bowls, below is the recipe for that.

Makes 4 mini bowls

Ingredients:

- 3oz. Lean ground beef, cooked and drained
- 1 tablespoon salsa
- 1/4 Mexican cheese
- 1 diced avocado
- Diced olives (optional)

Directions:

Cook ground beef and salsa until meat is brown; set on paper towel covered plate for 3 minutes. Prepare bowls same as you would a taco. Serve and enjoy.

Nutritional Information:

- Sodium: 187 mg
- Potassium: 321 mg
- Calcium: 66 mg
- Protein: 18 g

Buttery Fettucine

Try different shapes and sizes pasta for something new and different!

Makes 1 cup

Ingredients:

- 8 oz. fettucine
- 1 tablespoon melted butter
- 1/2 tablespoon chopped oregano
- Juice of 1/2 lemon (optional)

Directions:

Cook fettucine for 8 minutes until al dente, drain but do not rinse. Melt butter with chopped oregano and pour over fettucine.

Nutritional Information:

- Sodium: 32 mg
- Potassium: 119 mg
- Calcium: 32 mg
- Protein: 14 g

Turkey and Coconut Broccoli Curry

Also great as a risotto!

Makes 1 cup

- 3 oz. turkey meat
- 1 cup rice
- 1/2 cup water
- 1 tablespoon coconut milk
- 1/2 broccoli pieces
- 1/2 tablespoon turmeric

Directions:

In pot over medium high heat bring water to a boil and pour in rice, stir well. Add the remaining ingredients and let come to a boil.

Reduce heat, cover, and let simmer 28-30 minutes.

Stir often so rice does not stick to bottom of pot. Cook turkey to desired doneness.

Nutritional Information:

- Sodium: 37 mg
- Potassium: 253 mg
- Calcium: 34 mg
- Protein: 32 g

Onion and Pepper Fajitas

For extra flavor try some carrots!

Makes 2

Ingredients:

- 2 corn tortilla shells
- 1 sweet onion, caramelized
- 1 tablespoon Worcester sauce
- 1 tablespoon butter
- 2 bell peppers sliced lengthwise
- Lime juice (optional)

Directions:

Slice onions into strips, put into sauce pan along with Worcester sauce and butter; keep stirring until onions are brown-gold and very fragrant.

If desired warm peppers in leftover caramelization mixture. Make fajitas and enjoy.

Nutritional Information:

- Sodium: 40 mg
- Potassium: 38 mg
- Calcium: 24 mg
- Protein: 4 g

Cauliflower Mash Pineapple Chicken

Garbanzo beans also make a great mash!

Makes 1 cup

Ingredients:

- 1 cup cauliflower pieces
- 1/2 tablespoon olive oil
- 1 cup bok choy
- 2 boneless skinless chicken breasts
- 1/2 tablespoon pineapple juice
- 1 tablespoon low sodium soy sauce

Directions:

In plastic bag marinade chicken in pineapple juice and soy sauce overnight. Pour cauliflower pieces, olive oil, and bok choy into a food processor and puree.

Butterfly chicken and spoon 2 tablespoons of mash on chicken. Put it back together and cook in skillet over medium-high heat cook chicken until no longer pink or running juices.

Eating undercooked chicken can be hazardous to your health, always cook chicken until done.

Nutritional Information:

- Sodium: 199 mg
- Potassium: 435 mg
- Calcium: 40 mg
- Protein: 28 g

Snacks and Side Dishes

Because we can't have rice crispy treats and cool whip
between every meal!

Spiced Corn

Great treat for all during and indoor or outdoor picnic!

Serves 4

Ingredients:

- 4 ears of corn
- 1 tablespoon of butter
- 1 tablespoon turmeric

Directions:

Prepare corn and grill. In microwave melt the butter, stir the turmeric into it, and with a sauce brush thoroughly coat each ear of corn.

Wrap in foil and place over medium flame 20-25 minutes, or cook without the foil for grill marks.

Nutritional Information:

- Sodium: 41 mg
- Potassium: 542 mg
- Calcium: 12 mg
- Protein: 20 g

Chipotle Mustard Greens

A great comfort food for a rainy weekend!

Makes 1 serving, 1 cup

Ingredients:

- 1 cup 4.5 oz. chopped mustard greens
- 2-3 cups water
- 2 teaspoon chili powder
- 1/4 teaspoon black pepper
- 1 tablespoon dry white wine or white cooking wine

Directions:

In pot empty mustard greens, water, chili powder, pepper, and wine; bring to a boil while stirring frequently. Reduce heat to low and let simmer 30-45 minutes.

Nutritional Information:

- Sodium: 29 mg
- Potassium: 305 mg
- Calcium: 109 mg
- Protein: 4 g

Rainy Day Beans

While beans are high in protein and iron but are also high in phosphorous, therefore, we suggest that you only enjoy these occasionally, when your numbers are good and as a 'treat'.

Serves 2

Ingredients:

- 1/2 pound Great Northern Beans
- 3-4 cups water
- 3 coarsely chopped parsley leaves (dried can be substituted)
- 3 basil leaves (dried can be substituted)
- 1 sprig of oregano (dried can be substituted)
- 1 teaspoon smoked paprika (Hungarian paprika can be sub.)
- 1/4 teaspoon black pepper

Directions:

Soak beans overnight this eases digestion. Empty into pot along with water, parsley, basil, oregano, paprika, and pepper; bring to boil stirring frequently, reduce heat to low and let simmer 2-3 hours.

if low sodium bacon, turkey bacon, or ham is had pieces can be added to bean mix for extra seasoning.

Nutritional Information:

- Sodium: 5 mg
- Potassium: 527 mg
- Calcium: 142 mg
- Protein: 18 g

Green Beans an Tofu

Tofu is high in potassium, even though you will most likely consume only a few pieces, do yourself a favor and be mindful of the totality of what you're eating and your numbers. Let this delicious side dish be a 'treat'!

Serves 3

Ingredients:

- 1 can, 14.5 oz., no salt added green beans
- 1/2 shallot diced
- 3 oz. Firm tofu, cubed and dried
- 1/3 cup water
- 1 tablespoon dry white wine or white cooking wine
- 1 tablespoon raw organic honey
- 1/2 tablespoon low sodium soy sauce
- 1 teaspoon red pepper flakes

Directions:

Empty all contents into pot, over high heat bring to a boil while stirring frequently. Reduce heat to low and simmer for 30-45 minutes.

Nutritional Information:

- Sodium: 87 mg
- Potassium: 266 mg
- Calcium: 585 mg
- Protein: 14 g

Candied Pineapple Bites

Makes strawberry and cherry too!

Makes 24

Ingredients:

- 1 vanilla cake mix, eliminate any added white sugar
  1/2 cup brown sugar
- 1/3 cup raw organic honey
- 2 finely chopped mint leaves
- 1 can pineapple, crushed

Directions:

Prepare 11x8 casserole dish or silicon brownie molds and preheat oven to temp stated on cake mix. In bowl mix together brown sugar, honey, mint, and pineapple and refrigerate until ready for it; in separate bowl make cake mix according to package directions.

Once ready, fill molds or dish with cake mix and spoon pineapple mixture on top; cook according to package directions.

Nutritional Information:

- Sodium: 73 mg
- Potassium: 398 mg
- Calcium: 113 mg
- Protein: 5 g

Spinach Chips:

Spinach can be high in calcium so keep up with your intake numbers!

Makes: 25-30

Ingredients:

- 1 bag of spinach or fresh spinach leaves chopped
- Olive oil for drizzling
- No-salt seasoning

Directions:

Prepare baking tray and preheat oven to 400. Layout spinach in small mounds about 1 inch apart, then drizzle with olive oil and sprinkle with seasoning. Bake 18-22 minutes.

Nutritional Information:

- Sodium: 24 mg
- Potassium: 168 mg
- Calcium: 30 mg
- Protein: 1 mg

Veggie Dip

Serve with carrot or celery sticks!

Makes 1 cup

Ingredients:

- 3 oz. cream cheese
- 1-2 diced basil leaves
- 1 teaspoon red pepper flakes

Directions:

Lay out cream cheese and let soften. Mix with basil and red pepper flakes; it will keep in the refrigerator in an air tight container.

Nutritional Information:

- Sodium: 671 mg
- Potassium: 7 mg
- Calcium: 152 mg
- Protein: 15 g

Apple Pie Crumble in a Cup

Serve with a bit of vanilla ice cream or your fav sherbet!

Makes 12

Ingredients:

- 1 vanilla angel food cake mix, homemade
- 4-6 large cooking apples diced, low sodium
- 2 tablespoon honey
- 1 teaspoon lemon juice
- Apple pie spice

Directions:

Prepare crockpot and mix cake mix; pour half in the bottom of crockpot. In separate bowl mix together apples, honey, and lemon juice; spread 1/2 apple mixture evenly on top of cake mix.

Continue with pattern until both mixes are gone and sprinkle with apple pie spice.

Bake 4 hours, the first two on low the last two on high.

Baked Chicken Taquitos with Fiesta Sauce

Try them with different homemade sauces!

Makes 6 roll-ups

Ingredients:

- 6 corn tortillas
- 1 boneless, skinless chicken breasts or thigh
- 1/4 cheddar cheese
- 1 cup no sodium diced tomatoes
- 1 teaspoon chili powder
- 1/3 teaspoon cumin
- 1/2 teaspoon celery salt or celery flakes
- 1 tablespoon lemon juice
- 1 chopped mint leaf (optional)

Directions:

Bake chicken for 1 hour; let sit for 12 minutes and shred or chop. Lay flat tortillas, place chicken and cheese down one side and roll.

Bake in 400 degree oven 8-10 minutes; meanwhile, mix together tomatoes, chili powder, cumin, celery salt or flakes, and lemon juice.

Nutritional Information:

- Sodium: 987 mg
- Potassium: 321 mg
- Calcium: 130 mg
- Protein: 40 g

5 Alarm Chicken Wings

Add beans and make a chicken chili to enjoy on those cold days!

Makes 6-8 wings

Ingredients:

- 6-8 chicken wings or drumets
- 1 cup molasses
- 3/4 cup ketchup
- 1 tablespoon mustard
- 1 teaspoon tabasco sauce
- 3 teaspoon cayenne power
- 1 teaspoon turmeric
- 1 diced habanero pepper

Directions:

In sauce pan combine all ingredients except for wings, stir and let simmer for 35 minutes.

While sauce is cooling place clean dry wings into crockpot and pour ½ of sauce over them.

With tongs or large spoon move wings around, ensuring all are coated; store remaining sauce in air tight container in refrigerator. Bake on high 1.5-2.5 hours.

considering using a cover for the inside since the sauce is messy and can stain

Nutritional Information:

- Sodium: 874 mg
- Potassium: 325 mg
- Calcium: 132 mg
- Protein: 32 g

Appetizers

Healthy food can be enjoyed by everyone!

Lasagna Rolls

Avoid worry or anxiety and eat these on low calcium days!

Makes 1 serving

Ingredients:

- 1 ciabatta roll cut in half
- 1 teaspoon olive oil
- 1 tablespoon skim milk ricotta cheese
- 1 basil leaf, chopped
- 1 large tomato diced
- 1 sprig of mint (optional)

Directions:

Turn on broiler. Separate roll and drizzle olive over half. Spread with ricotta cheese, top that with the chopped basil lay the tomato squares over the basil.

Cook under broiler for 3-5 minutes. Cut between the tomato squares to make bit-sized appetizers.

Nutritional Facts:

- Sodium: 734 mg
- Potassium: 70mg
- Calcium: 48 mg
- Protein: 17 g

Mac n' Cheese Muffins

A healthy party treat, makes 24 muffins.

Ingredients:

- 8 oz. rotini, penne, or small shell pasta
- 1 cup coconut milk
- 2 teaspoon nutritional yeast
- 1 oz. cream cheese
- 1 tablespoon parmesan cheese
- 1 tablespoon Monterey jack or pepper jack cheese
- 1 finely diced red bell pepper (optional)
- 2 finely diced mint leaves (optional, parsley or rosemary will work also)
- 1/3 cup cornflakes breadcrumbs

Directions:

Prepare muffin tins and preheat oven to 400. Fix pasta according to package directions for 7 minutes or until al dente. Drain but do not rinse.

In sauce pan bring to a boil milk, nutritional yeast and cheeses. Remove from heat and let cool; if using additions such as red peppers or mint add to milk mixture now.

Let sit 3-4 minutes, sauce will thicken and pour into pasta. If adding any vegetables such as broccoli, mushrooms, butternut squash, etc. now is the time to do that. Mix together and pour into muffin tin approx. 1/3- 1/2 full. Top with cornflakes breadcrumbs and bake 18-20 minutes.

Nutritional Information:

- Sodium: 822 mg
- Potassium: 68.7 mg
- Calcium: 322.9 mg
- Protein: 25.6

Shrimp Won Tons

Also great as a vegetarian treat!

Makes 12-14

Ingredients:

- 3 oz. medium-large shrimp cleaned, deveined and de-tailed
- 1 chopped bok choy
- 1/2 cup beansprouts
- 1 tablespoon of grated or minced ginger
- 1 tablespoon Worcester sauce
- 1/2 teaspoon orange peel

Directions:

Combine all ingredients into a food processor and pulse 15-20 seconds on low or a few quick pulses on high (if you end up with a soup or puree you have gone too far).

Layout Won Ton wrappers and spoon mixture into center, seal edges with water, and cook in oil until golden in color.

Nutritional Information:

- Sodium: 598 mg
- Potassium: 289 mg
- Calcium: 167 mg
- Protein:23 mg

Chicken Bites

Also great with turkey!

Makes 12

- 1 cups corn meal, corn masa, corn tortilla mix
- 1/2 water
- 1 can 14 oz. crushed tomatoes
- 2 teaspoons chili powder
- 3 oz. shredded chicken, cooked
- 1 teaspoon chopped parsley or oregano

Directions:

Prepare molds and preheat oven to 350. In bowl mix together corn masa and water; form dough into ball than knead on a floured surface for 4-8 minutes or until dough like consistency is a achieved. Press into the bottom of the molds.

In another bowl mix together tomatoes and spices; spoon on top of corn masa. Top with shredded turkey and any other ingredients you are using. Cook 28-32 minutes.

If mix needs more water add 1 teaspoon at a time.

Nutritional Information:

- Sodium: 438 mg
- Potassium: 128 mg
- Calcium: 67 mg
- Protein: 24 g

Veggie Spring Rolls

Try putting different spices like basil or thyme on these!

Makes 5

Ingredients:

- 5 rice paper wrappers
- 1 cup carrot matchsticks
- 1 cup sliced cucumber
- 1 cup dice celery stalk
- 1 cup beansprouts1 cup lettuce, spinach, or kale (optional)
- 1 cup sour cream
- 2 tablespoon parsley

Directions:

In a bowl mix together sour cream and parsley, refrigerate when done. Layout wrappers and spread evenly amongst them the veggies. Spread with sour cream mixture or use as a dip.

Nutritional Information:

- Sodium: 324 mg
- Potassium: 32 mg
- Calcium: 34 mg
- Protein: 9 g

Hummus Zest

Great dip for wraps too!

Makes 1 cup

Ingredients:

- 1 cup low sodium chickpeas
- 1 tablespoon olive oil or coconut oil
- 1 teaspoon orange peel
- 1 teaspoon chopped oregano
- 1/2 teaspoon thyme
- 1/4 teaspoon cumin
- 1/4 teaspoon celery salt or celery flakes

Directions:

Combine all ingredients in food processor and blend.

Nutritional Information:

- Sodium: 129 mg
- Potassium: 236 mg
- Calcium: 198 mg
- Protein: 13 g

Baked Tortilla Chips and Homemade Salsa

Garlic powder is lower than garlic salt in sodium but be sure to read all labels before buying!

Makes 24 chips and 1 cup salsa

Ingredients:

- 4 corn tortillas
- Olive oil
- Garlic powder (optional)
- 1 cup diced tomatoes
- 1 tablespoon lemon juice
- 2 teaspoon chili powder
- 1 teaspoon cumin
- 1 teaspoon onion powder

Directions:

Prepare baking tray and preheat oven to 425. Cut tortilla shells into sixths, making six individual triangles out of each tortilla round.

Layout on tray and drizzle each piece with oil and sprinkle each piece with garlic powder if using. In a bowl mix together all other ingredients and serve.

Left over salsa can be stored for later use in an air tight container in the refrigerator.

Bake chips 12-14 minutes.

Zucchini Fries

A great alternative to greasy fries!

Makes 16

Ingredients:

- 1 zucchini
- 2 eggs whites
- 1/2 homemade or low sodium breadcrumbs
- 2 teaspoon paprika

Directions:

Prepare try and preheat oven to 425. Cut zucchini lengthwise into fry like shape; in a small bowl mix together egg whites and paprika.

In another bowl pour breadcrumbs, dip zucchini fries in egg mixture, roll in breadcrumbs, and bake 8-12 minutes.

Nutritional Information:

- Sodium: 238 mg
- Potassium: 384 mg
- Calcium: 87 mg
- Protein: 24 g

Chicken Salad Celery Sticks

Try it on carrots and cucumbers too!

Makes 8

Ingredients:

- 2 celery stalk each cut into 4 pieces
- 8 oz. cream cheese
- 1 teaspoon parsley
- 1 tablespoon minced ginger
- 1/2 cup chicken pieces or cubes

Directions:

In a bowl mix soften cream cheese, parsley, ginger, and chicken. Spread dip into celery centers. Dip will stay if kept in an air tight container in the refrigerator.

Nutritional Information:

- Sodium: 487 mg
- Potassium: 387 mg
- Calcium: 234 mg
- Protein: 43 mg

Baked Shrimp Fritters

Find tapioca starch, along with other items to substitute for non-kidney diet foods in health food stores!

Makes 12

Ingredients:

- 1/2 pound medium shrimp, cleaned, deveined, and de-tailed
- 4 eggs whites
- 1 cup all-purpose flour
- 2 teaspoon tapioca starch
- 1/4 cup coconut milk
- 1 cup breadcrumbs
- 1/2 tablespoon thyme

Directions:

Prepare baking tray and preheat oven to 375.

Combine all ingredients, except for shrimp, into a bowl and mix well.

Chop up shrimp and fold into mixture, stir well.

Spoon mounds onto tray and bake 25-30 minutes.

Nutritional Information:

- Sodium: 684 mg
- Potassium: 386 mg
- Calcium: 324 mg
- Protein: 45 g

Helpful Tips

- ALWAYS COMPARE NUTRITIONAL LABELS

- SOMETIMES THE CHEAPEST IS THE BEST, EXPENSIVE DOES NOT ALWAYS EQUAL BETTER

- EATING HEALTHY DOES NOT AUTOMATICLY MEAN LONGER PREP TIMES OR COOKING TIMES

- TAKE THE TIME TO LEARN SPICES AND WHAT THEY CAN DO FOR YOU

- HEALTH IS NOT A LUXARY IT DOESN'T HAVE TO DRIVE YOU INTO THE POOR HOUSE

- IFYOU MUST BY A 'NORMAL' CANNED GOOD AND NOT A LOW SALT RUN IT UNDER COLD WATER FOR 1-3 MINUTES. THIS WILL WASH OFF A LOT OF THE FACTORY SEASONINGS WHICH ARE HIGH IN SODIUM.

- DOWNLOAD APPS TO HELP WITH PHOSPOHOUS AND VARIOUS NUTRITIONAL CONTENT

- FROZEN IS AS GOOD AS FRESH

- MAKE THE WEEKS SHOPPING LIST BEFORYOU GO

- PLAN MEALS AND SHOP FOR THEM IN ADVANCE

- DO NOT HATE YOURSELF FOR SLIP UPS, YOU'RE ONLY HUMAN, JUST GET BACK ON TRACK AS SOON AS POSSIBLE

- ALLOW YOURSELF OCCASIONAL TREATS, PREFERABLY AFTER LABS!!

**Nutritional Info provided by an Online Database,
Therefore, They are not to be taken as definite**

PLEASE DO YOUR OWN NUMERICAL FIGURING TO
INSURE THAT YOU STAY WITHIN YOUR DR.
PRESCRIBED RANGES AND MAINTAIN OPTIMAL
LEVELS OF HEALTH. Neither the author, publishing
company, nor book distributor take responsibility for
incorrect nutritional values or your failure to stay within
your nutritional levels or parameters; there are too many
variables including brand , sodium content, serving size,
etc. to calculate error free numbers for every recipe. Also,
remember that the nutritional info listed reflects the entire
recipe unless otherwise stated. Individual portion size is
usually 3 oz. to 1 cup but again that differs from person to
person, thus, is not possible to list. The figuring of this
number is your responsibility.

For dietary and shopping help there are numerous
resources, websites, and apps that are available for
download on your iPhone, apple, Microsoft, or android
devices. Enquire with your Drs., in-center dialysis staff or
dietician for further details.

Author's Afterthoughts

Thanks ever so much to each of my cherished readers for investing the time to read this book!

I know you could have picked from many other books but you chose this one. So a big thanks for downloading this book and reading all the way to the end.

If you enjoyed this book or received value from it, I'd like to ask you for a favor. Please take a few minutes to post an honest and heartfelt review on Amazon.com. Your support does make a difference and helps to benefit other people.

Thanks for your Reviews!

Gordon Rock
bunsomsaetow@gmail.com

57191704R00052

Made in the USA
Charleston, SC
08 June 2016